VISITING

THE

TOOTH

DOCTOR

Steven L. Haase, D.D.S.
(TOOTH FIXER)

Library of Congress Catalog Card Number: 94-12045
Haase, Steven L., 1960-
VISITING THE TOOTH DOCTOR / Steven L. Haase

Summary: A dentist tells children what happens at the dentist, with explanations of equipment and procedures and a section for parents.

ISBN 0-9631449-6-0
First Edition
1 2 3 4 5 6 7 8 9 10
1. Children--dental examinations--Juvenile literature

Printed in the United States of America
Published simultaneously in Canada
Wright & Co. Publishers, Incorporated
4839 E. Greenway Road, Suite 154
Scottsdale, AZ 85254
1-800-618-3619

This book is
dedicated
to
my daughter
Bianca,
who
taught me
the meaning
of
unconditional
love.

WORDS FROM OTHERS

"I feel this is a must read for all young children and their parents. The book addresses and explains all aspects of a child's visit to the dentist alleviating the fear of the unknown. Not only will the children benefit from this, the parents will learn as well. ... I was amazed at the amount of knowledge I gained by reading the book." – APRIL ERICKSON, 2/3 grade teacher, Aztec Elementary School

"Perfect for the dental office, home or school library, "Visiting the Tooth Doctor" is a marvelous book that takes the fear out of dentistry. Dr. Haase has given the entire profession a valuable, practical and successful answer to providing children with enjoyable and informative trips to the dentist." – DR. GARY SEVERANCE, Ivoclar North America, Inc.

"What this book does is makes children very comfortable with their dentists, it educates them on the importance of oral health as well as encourages them to fully participate and take responsibility for their own health. How can any person who truly cares about children and oral health not be interested in this book?" – IMTIAZ MANJI, President, ExperDent Consultants, Inc.

"My hat is off to Dr. Steve Haase, for his outstanding contribution to future generations. Perhaps this wonderful book will begin to break down centuries of dental myths and lead to the next generation to good oral hygiene. ,... It fills an urgent vacancy in dental education for both children and their parents." – HOWARD FARRAN, DDS, FAGD, President and CEO, Today's Dental

"As a professional counselor, I applaud your sensitivity to the children's fears and the unknown of visiting a dental office. The book communicated a warm personal message, enabling children of all ages to feel safe and secure while promoting dental health wellness. This book is a gift to be cherished by many children and families.' – BRENDA GARRETT, R.N., M.C., C.P.C., Psychological Counseling Services

"I am certain that in addition to reducing children's anxieties about medical procedures, this book will significantly reduce the anxiety level of parents as well! This is an excellent resource for the parents of preschoolers." – JULIA ANN DANIELS, Assistant Professor of Psychology, Central Michigan University

Foreword

I would like to thank Dr. Keith Martin, Wichita, Kansas, for all the love and the care he showed me as a child.

As I grew older, I always thought how wonderful it would be to treat patients the same way Dr. Martin treated me. I thought nothing could be greater than to have my own patients feel as comfortable and as fearless as I was at the dentist.

It was this memory that inspired me to become a dentist and helped me to develop patience, understanding, and the immense concern I have for my patients' comfort and well-being.

Thanks, Dr. Martin.

I wish to extend special

"THANKS"

to all of those helpful to me

in the completion of this book:

Jim Hanna - Denton Hanna Photography

Marge Mc Masters - Initial Editing

Angelen VanDaele - Graphic Design and Illustration

Bud Wright - Printing and Distribution

and

My Wonderful Staff and Patients - Inspiration

Thanks,

Contents

Introduction

Wow, it's time to go to the dentist and there are so many questions to ask. Why do I need to go? What's the dentist going to do? How many times will I go? Is it ok to be scared? Will it hurt? Is the dentist nice and will he or she be nice to me? Will the dentist listen to me and explain things to me so I can understand what's happening?

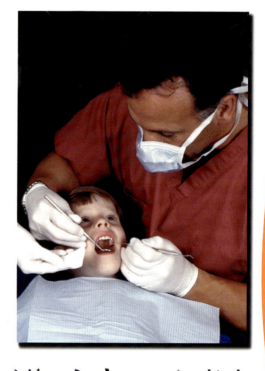

All of these questions are very, very important. I am a dentist and my name is Dr. Steven Haase (that's pronounced Hace). I am a dentist for many, many children. I have a seven-year old daughter, Bianca, whom I love more than the man in moon. (That's a lot!). I work on her teeth and she loves to go to the dentist.

I've written this book to hopefully answer all of your questions about going to the dentist and to make your trip to the dentist a fun and exciting time.

The following pages will help you understand what you can expect at the dentist's office. This book is full of neat-o-stuff that I think you will find very interesting.

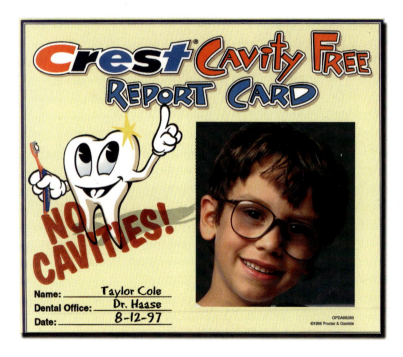

Have fun reading this and let's get started!

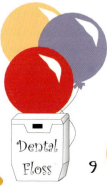

The Dentist

The dentist is a very, very smart person. In fact, the dentist has gone to many years of school to learn enough about your mouth and teeth to take care of them.

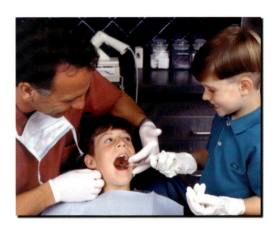

The dentist wants your teeth to be healthy so you can eat, drink, and talk easily and correctly. The dentist wants to make sure you're doing o.k. He or she will count your teeth, look at movie-star pictures of your teeth, and see if there are any tooth-bugs in your teeth that may make them hurt or look funny.

The dentist will answer all of your questions and tell you how your teeth are doing. You will also be taught how to brush and floss your teeth and how to take the best care of them.

Dental Floss

The dentist is a person you can trust, because you and your teeth are most important. When you are with the dentist, you are the only one the dentist cares about at that time. ONLY YOU!

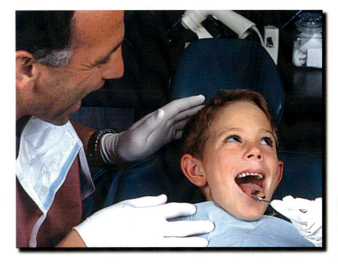

It is really neat to have your teeth counted by the dentist so you will know how many teeth you have. Wow! Did you know you are supposed to have twenty baby teeth and thirty-two big teeth? That's a bunch of teeth. Now you can ask your parents, teachers, and friends how many teeth they should have and see if they know the answer. Pretty cool, huh?

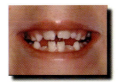

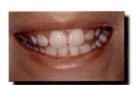

The Hygienist (tooth cleaner)

Usually before you see the dentist, you will see the person called the hygienist. This is the person who cleans your teeth and takes the movie-star pictures. In my office, the hygienist is a girl and she is really, really nice. She is very smart. She had to go to gobs and gobs of school just to learn how to clean your teeth and how to take movie-star pictures.

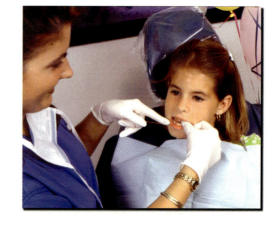

She usually uses a little squirt gun to squirt your teeth and get them wet. This really tickles and will probably make you laugh. She uses a really cool tooth tickler that tickles off all of the yucky PLAQUE on your teeth. Plaque is the yucky white stuff on the sides of your teeth. Lots of times, kids just like you laugh a lot because it tickles and is lots of fun. That's o.k.! It's pretty neat-o.

Sometimes the hygienist will use this red stuff to show us where the plaque is. It turns your tongue red and looks real cool.

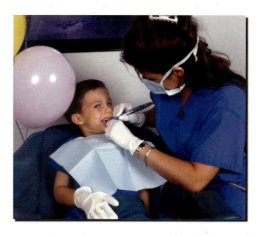

After she cleans your teeth and makes them look beautiful, she shows you how to brush your teeth and gives you a new toothbrush and floss so that yucky plaque won't come back. That's really nice of her to do that. She does this because she really, really cares about you and your teeth.

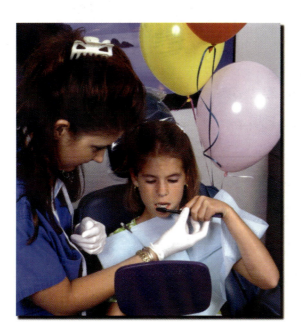

Dental Floss

The Assistants and Staff

The assistants are the dentist's most important helpers. In my office, the assistants are all girls. They are very smart. They have to learn a whole bunch of stuff so they can help the dentist when he or she is working in your mouth.

The dentist could not work very well without the dental assistants. The dental assistants are really nice and really care about making you and your teeth happy and comfortable.

They make sure you and everything is all right all of the time. They take movie-star pictures and they usually sit right beside you at all times in case you need something.

They use the squirt gun in your mouth, and give your teeth a bath. They use a really cool straw like a tiny vacuum cleaner to get all of the extra water and stuff out of your mouth. They use lots of cool things like magic blue lights for your teeth, tooth pillows (cotton), tiny mirrors and even "Tooth Fairy" boxes. Wow!

In our office, the dental assistants turn the television on for you to see cartoons. After the dentist is finished, they take you to the toy box and get you some helium balloons. Isn't that really nice? Everyone really likes the dental assistants. They are very important in the dental office.

Toybox (Very Cool)

Dental Floss

The Stuff We Wear

You probably wonder why we wear all those funny-looking clothes. Well, we wear all those funny-looking clothes and things to protect us and you from bad germs

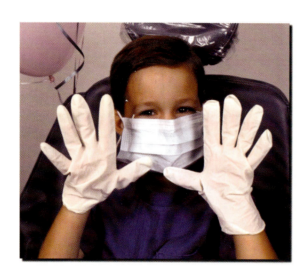

and stuff like that. The clothes that look like pajamas are called "SCRUBS." Wow, that is an unusual name. Scrubs are worn to keep us from getting germs from you and your mouth onto our skin and good clothes. Scrubs are very comfortable and make us feel like we're wearing our pajamas to work. It's really neat.

We also wear a thing over our faces called a MASK. It's like covering your mouth when you cough, except with a mask, we don't need to use our hand. Instead, the MASK stops your germs from getting onto our faces and stops

our germs from getting onto you. It's like
Halloween all the time. With the mask on, we can
still breathe and talk.

Next, we'll talk about GLOVES. We wear gloves
to keep yucky stuff off our hands. This helps prevent the spread of germs, and with gloves, we won't
give you our yucky germs either. The gloves are made
of a material called latex. This comes from special

trees. That's pretty cool if you ask me! The gloves
keep all the water and stuff off our skin. These
gloves can stretch like a balloon.
Sometimes in my office, we blow
the gloves up like a balloon and draw
a face on it. We call it "Balloon
Man." You should ask your dentist
to do this. It looks really funny!

Many times the dentist and staff will wear funny-looking glasses called GOGGLES or SAFETY GLASSES. These are to protect the eyes from getting stuff in them. This way the dentist can always see you very well. These glasses are made of a very hard material so they won't break.

Sometimes all this stuff can look very scary if you don't know what it is. Now you know what this stuff is for and you won't have to be scared. Instead, pretend the dentist is dressed up for Halloween.

Take time to look at the pictures of this stuff so you will know exactly what it is when you see it. If you ask, your dentist may give you a mask and gloves to take home with you. Wouldn't that be great?

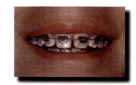

Dental Floss

Your Feelings

Your feelings and thoughts are most important to us at the dental office. We know many of you may

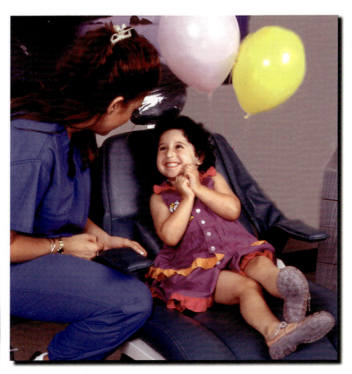

be worried and nervous about being at the dentist's office.

This is perfectly normal and we understand. After you have read this book and have been to the dentist, you won't need to be frightened. We will always try to tell you everything that we are going to do before we do it so you will be comfortable.

Usually, you go to the dentist to get your teeth cleaned, checked, and counted. This allows us to know if you have any problems in your mouth that need to be fixed.

If there are any problems, such as toothbugs, etc., we want to find them early so they don't eat your teeth. We will talk more about toothbugs later in the book.

Any questions you may have are very, very important to us. We want your visit to the dentist to be fun and exciting so you can tell all of your friends how much fun you had. We will always listen to you and explain what's happening at all times in a way you can understand. If you want, your mom or dad can be there with you. You can decide that.

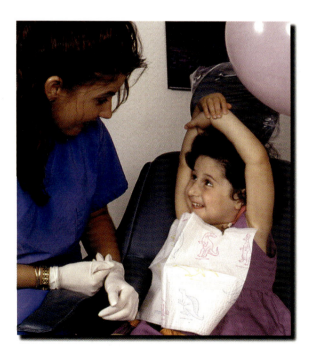

Dental Floss

Your Mouth

Your mouth is made up of many different parts. You have a tongue which is mainly used to taste your food. Those little tiny round things on top are called TASTE BUDS. These help you decide what food tastes like. That's really cool. Your tongue also helps you talk correctly. What would we do without a tongue?

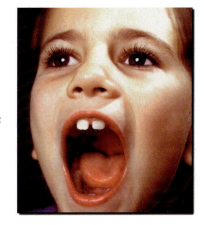

Next are your teeth. Did you know that you are supposed to have twenty (20) baby teeth? That's right, twenty. As you grow older, you will lose those twenty teeth and you will get big teeth. These are called permanent teeth and you normally should get thirty-two (32) of these. Wow!

That is a bunch of teeth. You probably are wondering where they all will fit. Well, as you grow older and bigger, so does your mouth and gum area. This allows the teeth to fit. Sometimes there isn't enough

room for all of the teeth and you will have to get braces. I (DR. HAASE) had braces because there just wasn't enough room for all of my teeth. I am sure glad I was lucky enough to get braces. Now I have straight teeth and a nice smile.

Also, there are those flappy things in front of your teeth. They are called LIPS. Your lips are very important in keeping everything in your mouth and helping you talk the correct way. Always wear sun block on your lips when outside. You need those lips.

The top of your mouth sounds like part of a house. The top is called the ROOF or PALATE. The bottom area is called the FLOOR. The areas on the sides are called the CHEEKS. These help us keep food in our mouth while chewing and they also help us talk. You probably know this, but you can blow your cheeks out like a balloon. I wonder if they could POP like a balloon?

The watery stuff in our mouth is called SALIVA. That's a pretty big word. Say it again .... SA-LI-VA. Great! Saliva is very, very important for many reasons. First, it helps us digest our food when we eat and swallow. Secondly, it keeps the teeth wet and this helps fight off toothbugs (cavities). This is most important. We really need saliva. This is the stuff on your pillow in the morning.

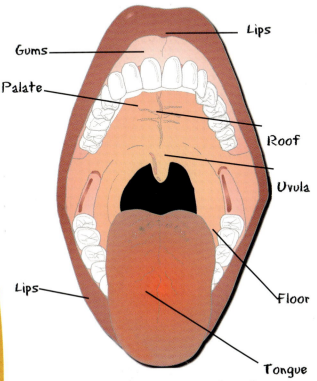

Gums
Palate
Lips
Roof
Uvula
Floor
Lips
Tongue

Last, we usually have a long thing sticking down from the top-back area of our mouth. This is called the UVULA. Sometimes it is really long like a worm and sometimes it is very short.

All of the parts of the mouth are equally important. They (the parts) all work together to help you eat, drink, breathe and talk; not necessarily in that order.

So, when you visit the dentist, he or she checks all of these areas, not just your teeth.

Dental Floss

Your Teeth

Your teeth are such amazing things. Not only do they chew your food, they do many more things. The teeth can feel hot or cold in your mouth. Your teeth help you talk correctly and chew your food well.

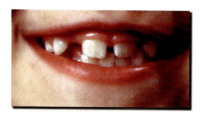

Tooth

Did you know that different teeth in your mouth are used for different things? They are! Your front teeth are called the INCISORS. That's pronounced "in-si-zers." These teeth are used to cut your food before you swallow it. You usually have eight (8) of these in baby teeth and in permanent teeth. Next, you have the eye teeth, which are called the CANINE teeth. These teeth are usually the longest teeth in your mouth and are used for holding and tearing your food while eating it.

Usually, you will have two (2) on top and two (2) on bottom. That equals four (4) altogether. You should have

these in baby teeth and in permanent teeth. Last, your
back teeth are PREMOLARS and MOLARS. These are
strong teeth used to chew and mash your food so you
can swallow it. You have eight (8) baby molars and twelve
(12) permanent molars along
with eight (8) permanent
premolars. The premolars are
the permanent teeth just in
front of the molars.

I know this seems like a
lot of teeth, but you need all
of the teeth you get. Can
you imagine not having teeth?
You usually get your baby
teeth between six months
and one year of age. You
continue getting your baby
teeth until you have twenty teeth. You should get your
front teeth first.

Usually, your bottom front teeth come
in first, followed by your top front teeth.
After your baby teeth have been in awhile,
you should get your permanent teeth.
Usually, you get your permanent first molars

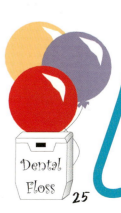

Dental
Floss

in back around the time you lose your front baby teeth. After this, you will get your permanent front teeth.

Occasionally, the order in which we get our teeth may change, but don't be concerned with this unless your teeth don't come in at all. If this happens, your dentist should take a look. You should get a total of thirty-two (32) permanent teeth. WOW!

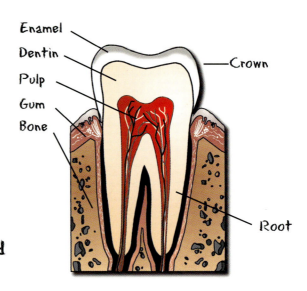

Enamel
Dentin
Pulp
Gum
Bone
Crown
Root

There are lots of parts to the teeth. The top part of the tooth is called the CROWN. The bottom part is called the ROOT and usually cannot be seen. The outside part of a tooth is called the ENAMEL. Did you know enamel is the hardest part of the human body? It is the hard white part we see when we look at the teeth. The inside part is called the DENTIN. We usually cannot see this part. The part way inside is called the PULP or NERVE. The nerve is what helps tell your brain when you have a toothache.

Dental Floss

26

Movie-Star Pictures (X-rays)

When you go to the dentist, usually you will have MOVIE-STAR pictures taken. These are pictures taken of all your teeth. Every tooth gets to act like a movie-star.

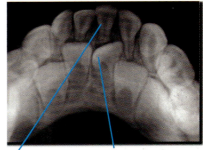

Baby Tooth   Permanent Tooth
                  ready to come up!

These pictures are sometimes called X-rays, but WE call them movie-star pictures. It's really cool to see your teeth on pictures. These pictures show all of the tooth. They show the roots, the enamel, the nerve and even any toothbugs that may be on your teeth.

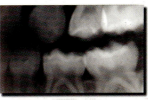

This is important so the dentist can make sure your teeth are in perfect shape. With these movie-star pictures, your permanent or big-person teeth can be seen before they come into your mouth. That is really neat.

The next time you go to the dentist, ask if you can get some movie-star pictures of your teeth.

Plaque (yuck)

Wow, what a yucky word! Well, plaque is that yucky, white stuff that gets on your teeth. When you wake up in the morning, take your fingernail and scrape the bottom of your teeth. You will probably get white, creamy-like stuff off of your teeth.

This is PLAQUE!

Plaque is made up of food and germs. It usually builds up on the teeth and can cause toothbugs (cavities) and BAD BREATH! Sometimes it is hard to see plaque and that is why you have to brush your teeth very well every time. Plaque also gets on your tongue. If you brush your tongue, you can get this "YUCKY" plaque off.

Sometimes, the dentist will have you chew up these funny little red tablets. This is really fun because it turns the

28

plaque red. When the plaque turns red, you can see it very easily and then it can be removed with your toothbrush.

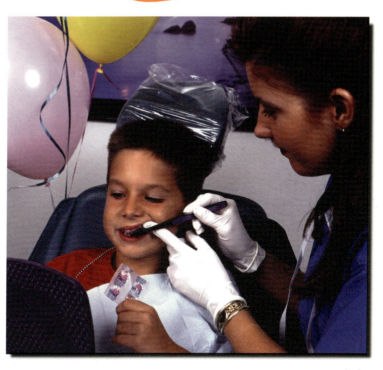

Sometimes, even mom and dad use the red tablets to see the plaque and remove it. The red looks cool.

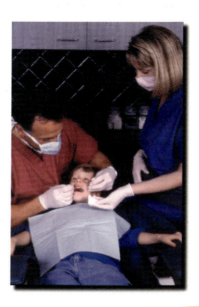

Toothbugs = (cavities)

Sometimes your teeth get TOOTH BUGS or CAVITIES. This can happen for many reasons. Sometimes teeth aren't perfect and small holes can

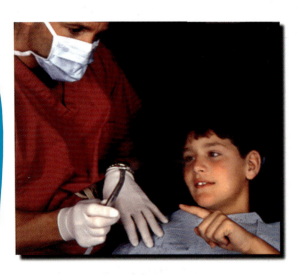

occur when the teeth are made. If this happens, toothbugs or (cavities) can form in these areas.

If we don't brush our teeth and keep them clean, the plaque will stay on our teeth and this can cause toothbugs. Also, we eat LOTS OF SUGAR! SUGAR is the MAIN reason we get toothbugs.

Dental Floss

What are TOOTHBUGS? Toothbugs aren't really bugs like we see outside; instead, they are like very, very small germs that sit on the tooth and start

30

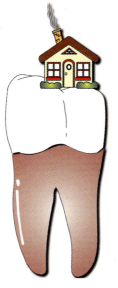

Sugar sets up a house in your mouth for the toothbugs!

to grow until it makes a hole or (cavity) in the tooth. Once this happens, the cavity just gets bigger and bigger until it hurts your tooth. When the dentist finds toothbugs on one of your teeth, he or she will tell you and your mom or dad. You can return to the dentist and have the toothbugs removed before they eat too much of your tooth. In my office, I show boys and girls their toothbugs on a big camera, if possible. Sometimes, they look pretty weird.

If your dentist says you have toothbugs, don't worry, just be glad they were found before they ate your tooth. Toothbugs are easily removed.

"Now, whose mouth am I going to call home today?"

Sleepy Juice (shots)

Sleepy juice is what the dentist uses to put the toothbugs to sleep so they can be removed without hurting. Once the toothbugs are sleeping, they are removed and hopefully gone forever.

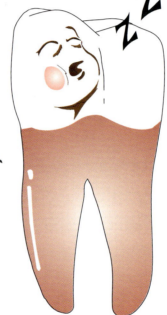

Sleepy juice makes your mouth feel really, really weird for a little while. It makes your tongue and lips go to sleep. When this happens, your tongue and lips

feel like they aren't on your face for a little while.

Sometimes, we listen to hear if the toothbugs are
sleeping before we
remove them. We try to
hear if the toothbugs
are "snoring" or not.
What do you think about
that?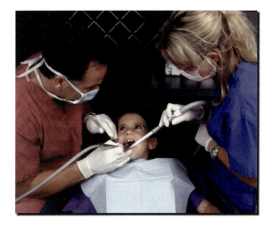

Sometimes the sleepy juice may give you a very,
very little, teensy-weensy "pinch" just at first. This
is no big deal. After that, it's really easy!

When the sleepy juice wears off, it feels very
tingly and sometimes a little "itchy". This usually goes
away pretty quickly.

Your dentist uses sleepy juice to
make removing the toothbugs easy, so
it doesn't hurt you. This is why sleepy
juice is so good to use.

Dental
Floss

Toothbug Remover

The Toothbug Remover is kind of like a really neat "squirt gun" for the tooth. Once the toothbug is asleep, the toothbug remover is used to spray water on the tooth and rinse the toothbug away.

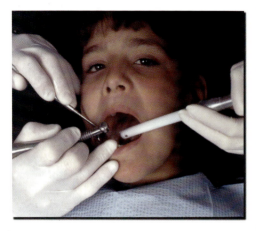

The toothbug remover is sometimes called the DRILL. Air and water is blown through the toothbug remover and this is how the toothbug is removed. The toothbug remover, or the drill, makes a very high-pitched noise inside your mouth. At first, this may seem kind of scary, but it is just noise and it works very well to remove the toothbug.

Your mouth will get water in it while the toothbug remover is being used and the assistant will use her tiny tooth vacuum cleaner to suck the water out. It feels and sounds pretty weird.

After the toothbug is removed, the dentist will put a FILLING in the hole. We'll talk about that next.

Fillings

Once the toothbug is gone, there is usually a big hole in the tooth. If this hole is left open, your tooth will hurt once the sleepy juice wears off. To make sure your tooth doesn't hurt, the dentist puts in what we call a FILLING. The filling is put inside the hole and it gets very, very hard so you can chew on it just like your tooth. There are many different types of fillings. Some are silver and are pushed into the hole. With these types of fillings, you may hear a "squeaky" sound in the tooth while the dentist puts it in. Once it gets hard in the tooth, the dentist polishes it and makes it shiny.

Another type of filling is called a COMPOSITE. That's said like "com-pos-it." It is a filling that looks just like your tooth and is the only kind we use in my dental office. Once the composite is placed in the tooth, the assistant uses what we call a "magic" blue light and shines it on the filling.

35

This "magic" blue light is what makes the new filling really, really hard. Once the composite has hardened, the dentist uses the drill to smooth and polish it. After this is done, the new filling looks just like your tooth. Wow, isn't that cool?

Sometimes if the hole is really big, we may use other fillings that smell funny. We don't use these very often unless the toothbug has made a big, big hole. Don't worry if you smell something funny. Just remember, it will help your tooth feel better.

Sometimes, if the hole in your tooth is really, REALLY, REALLY big, the dentist will use what we call a TOOTH RING. This tooth ring fits around your tooth to help keep the filling material from moving until the dentist can finish fixing your tooth.

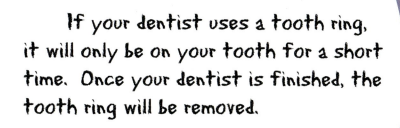

If your dentist uses a tooth ring, it will only be on your tooth for a short time. Once your dentist is finished, the tooth ring will be removed.

If your tooth is broken or badly decayed, your dentist may use what we call a CROWN. A crown is like putting a hat on the head of the tooth. This

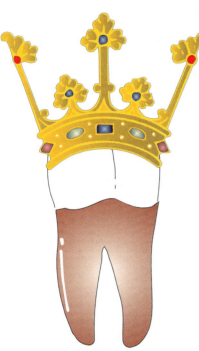

helps cover the top of your tooth so it will not break and hurt you. It's like putting a hat on to keep your head dry. Isn't that a great idea?

Some crowns are white like your tooth and some are silver like a shiny nickel. Either way, they work great to keep your tooth safe.

So, as you can see, there are a lot of ways to fix your teeth. Whatever way your dentist chooses, you should feel very, very lucky you are able to have your teeth fixed. Your dentist will fix them in the best possible way!

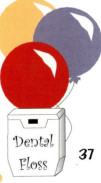

Sealants and Fluoride

Wow, these sound like really big words. Actually, they are big words and are pronounced as follows: "SEAL-ANTS" and "FLOR-IDE."

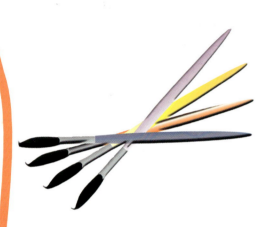

Sealants are like a "magic" paint we put on all of your back teeth to prevent toothbugs. Usually the assistants get your teeth really clean and dry. Next, they use a tiny paintbrush to paint the sealant onto the top of your teeth. After this, they use the "magic" blue light to harden the sealant. This is really, really easy and doesn't hurt at all.

While this is done, the assistants use a lot of soft cotton (We call these... "tooth pillows") beside your

teeth to help keep them totally dry. This doesn't take very long and it is very important to keep your mouth really WIDE OPEN while the sealants are being put on your teeth.

You are VERY lucky if you get sealants. With sealants, you may not get any toothbugs. That is totally cool!!!!!

Fluoride is the stuff the hygienist puts onto your teeth after they are cleaned. It works very well to help stop toothbugs. Sometimes it tastes funny, but it is very good for your teeth. If your hygienist uses fluoride on your teeth, you should be very glad.

Sometimes fluoride tablets are chewed every day to help make your teeth strong and keep the toothbugs away. These taste good; like candy. They should only be taken when mom or dad gives them to you.

Nowadays, with the help of SEALANTS and FLUORIDE, many boys and girls are growing up without any toothbugs or cavities. If your dentist tells mom or dad that you need either of these, you will be very lucky and hopefully you will grow up without toothbugs!

Dental Floss

Medicines

It may be necessary for you to take some medicine to help your tooth feel better. If the toothbug or cavity causes an OUCHY or toothache, this medicine is taken to fight the germs or to help make the ouchy feel better.

Medicine is easy to take and it will help you feel better. It is very, very important to take the medicine exactly as your dentist and your parents tell you to take it.

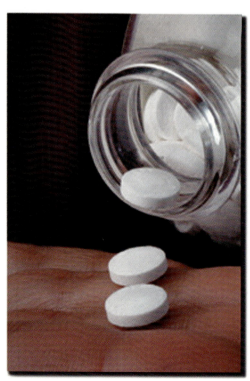

Dental Floss

The TOY BOX (FINISHED)

In my office, every boy and girl gets to go to the TOY BOX when the work on their teeth is finished. This is pretty exciting because we have a great toy box! It gives you something to look forward to when you're done. Neat-o!

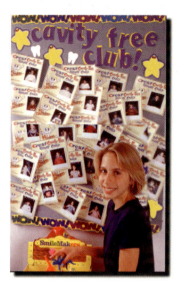

Usually the hygienist or assistants give you a bunch of helium balloons in my office. This is pretty cool too!

Your dentist may do different things to thank you for a job well done. He or she is very thankful for you being a grown-up boy or girl while in the office.

Now that you have read this book, you are ready for a visit to the dentist or TOOTH DOCTOR. You don't have to worry about what will happen once you are there because YOU ALREADY KNOW!

Mom and Dad

I would like to say thanks for reading this book and sharing it with your child or children. It is very important to introduce a child to the world of dentistry at an early age. In my practice, I encourage parents to 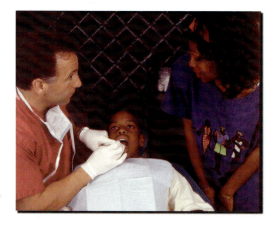 start between the age of two-and-a-half or three years of age, depending on the individual child.

We proceed very slowly at the child's pace during the first or second visits. For some, it takes a couple of visits to help a child feel comfortable. Whatever the circumstance, we never create an atmosphere of fear, guilt, or shame at the child's expense.

We are dealing with a new, unknown experience in a young child's life. THIS IS IMPORTANT TO THE CHILD AND TO THE PARENT. With this in mind, we do our best to keep the atmosphere positive and encouraging.

Children are very, very intuitive and can sense their parent's anxieties as well as feeling their own. Many

times, parents create a negative impression of the dentist before the child ever sets foot in the office. This occurs in a child's mind each time a subtle psychological leverage is used on the child; such as, "If you don't brush your teeth, you'll have to go to the "dentist!", or, "If you eat all of that sugar, you're going to get CAVITIES and have to go to the dentist!" Immediately, the child assumes the "dentist" must be a bad thing or mom and dad wouldn't use this as leverage. It is important to create positive impressions concerning your child's dental health and dental visits.

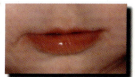

Furthermore, DON'T MAKE A BIG DEAL ABOUT GOING TO THE DENTIST! A child knows something is up when a great deal of a parent's energy is spent trying to convince him or her that a situation is really, really, really, really, really fun, fun, fun, fun. (If you get the idea.)

When you as parents go to the dentist for a cleaning and checkup, take your child and ask the dentist if it's

ok for your child to be present. This is done regularly in

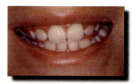

my office and allows the child to see how easy it is for mom or dad. The child is allowed to be an outsider at this point and is not thrown into the game as a player, but merely observes as a spectator. Afterwards, the child gets to go to the toy box for being "patient" and waiting for mom or dad. They think this is great! They leave thinking the dental office is a wonderful place and having positive thoughts.

I don't recommend a child's first experience, as mentioned above, being one accompanying a parent on any type of operative dental visit with anesthetic, drilling, etc. The child should accompany a parent on a routine cleaning appointment. This allows the child to meet the hygienist and dentist in a positive, non-invasive situation.

When a child visits a dentist for the first time as a patient, it's usually for a cleaning and examination. I recommend the parent come into the operatory with the child and then make an excuse to leave briefly, such as going to the bathroom, etc. This immediately builds

Dental Floss

an independence in the child and reinforces the idea of safety if mom or dad is willing to leave him or her there alone. Many times, the child assumes there is some sort of apprehension or underlying danger if mom or dad insists on smothering them in the operatory during this initial experience. Remember, CHILDREN ARE VERY INSTINCTIVE!

If the child refuses the movie-star pictures the first time, it's no problem. We always make a deal though, that next time we take x-rays. This works very well for both the child and us. It proves to the child that we are not gladiators. It shows the child we respect his or her boundaries and it allows the child to make an agreement on an adult level. The child leaves our office thinking he or she had some control of the situation and wasn't totally overwhelmed. Afterwards, he or she always gets to go to the toy box.

I never tell a child a lie. I explain everything I am going to do prior to doing it. This removes the fear of the unknown. If something is going to "pinch," I tell

them and show them on their arm. Now they know what
they will have to
handle without the
surprise. IT'S
ALL A TRUST
THING WITH
CHILDREN! It is
very important to
PUT ALL DIA-
LOGUE INTO
THEIR TERMS.

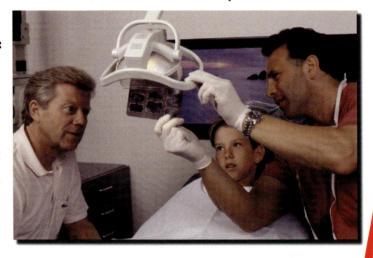

Regarding pre-treatment drugs, nitrous oxide,
and sedatives: I don't routinely use them. Some
practitioners rely on these methods as an adjunct
to their pedodontic practice. There are rare occasions
when the above-mentioned methods must be used,
but they are very infrequent.

Parents, please use many of these suggestions in
this book to make going to the dentist
fun. The children are innocent and it is up
to us to build trust, understanding and
loving relationships with each and every
one of them.

Dental
Floss 46

What to Ask the Dentist

Keep in mind, this is your child and you are entitled to ask any question(s) you may have. Following is a list of questions you may want to ask the dentist. He or she will probably be glad you asked these questions and very happy to answer them.

What percentage of your practice is children?

Do you have children of your own?

Does your staff have children?

How is my child's mouth?

Are any restorations needed?

If so, do you use pre-treatment drugs?

Can I help the brushing and flossing in any way?

Do you use tooth-colored fillings instead of silver fillings?

Should I have my child on fluoride tablets or drops?

Should my child use plaque-disclosing tablets prior to brushing?

Should I have my child's teeth sealed?

How is my child brushing?

Is my child missing any teeth?

Does my child need braces?

Will you stop if my child says it hurts?

Does my child need any dietary changes?

DID YOU READ, "VISITING THE TOOTH DOCTOR?"

If you have any questions, feel free to contact
your dentist, The American Dental Association,
the American Pediatric Dental Association
or Dr. Haase. We are all here to help you.

Most of all,
thanks!